In Loving Memory of Dad...

Furman H. Beck Sr.

Dedication

I thought long and hard about whom should be named on this page. I have so many strong feelings that go back a long way. I also think about all the families who were relocated, without having a say so into the move. I think that most just like me would never have left. They were happy just where they were... First, I would like to thank my family, my wife Linda of 49 years for her help and encouragement through this long process. I also want to thank my daughter Suzanne for her critical eye in proofing as well as my son Benji and my other daughter Sharon for their tireless efforts in helping put it all together. Then next would be my dear, lifelong friend Lois Williams Gleason and James (Jimmy) Cole. Then last but certainly not least, my Dad, Furman H. Beck Sr. and my Grandpa, John W. Patterson as they are always with me in spirit. These two men had a lot of influence in molding and making me the person I am today. They both taught me the value of a job well done and to strive to do my very best in whatever I attempted. They, just like me, would never have left our little Garden of Eden.

Table Of Contents

How It All Began - Portman Shoals The Book

Where do I start? I have spent a part of each day since leaving the little settlement, Portman Shoals, reminiscing in my mind all the hills and hollows that I used to run up and down. The beauty of it all and now covered with acres and acres of water.

I have read many articles and publications regarding Lake Hartwell. I have been well informed as to its size and of all the wonderful amenities around its shores and all the restaurants and recreational facilities available.

Then it came to me that most of the people driving the Highway 24 corridor into Anderson, SC or I-85 North or South, as well as the thousands of people that enjoy this beautiful lake by boat or recreation each year do not have a clue as to what used to be underneath all that water! This is where my adventure began to try my best to help preserve the history of Portman Shoals and show how much of an impact it has had in the shaping of this area and on anyone who enjoys the beauty of Lake Hartwell. I have spent many hours trying to locate individuals from my past and doing research.

I have so many people to thank for helping me. I will mention a few who have put up with my relentless questions and probing into their past in digging for information...

The first is my good friend,

Lois Williams Gleason.

I can't remember a time in my life that her family has not been a part of our family in some way. She has a wealth of knowledge and has been so willing to pass it on.

The next person I'd like to thank is Robert (Bob) Hill. We have been friends for a long time and both collected Corvair cars long ago when they still put engines in the trunk of a car! He blew my mind with all the information he had and has been so open to share it.

The third would be my friend Jim Cole. His dad was the last superintendent at Portman. He has been so gracious in giving me information and sending me pictures.

From my past, other names started to surface. These include Forrest Cole, Larry Palmer, Carl Patterson and Harold Grant to mention a few. Their vivid stories, pictures and memories have truly been a blessing to work with and I thank each and every one of you for so humbly lending me your time.

Portman Shoals

Through The Eyes Of A 10 Year Old

Pictured above is a happy kid that spent his days roaming throughout the little village called Portman Shoals. Never in my wildest dreams did I ever think I would have to leave this place. I couldn't fathom anyone in their right mind ever wanting to depart. We had everything a person could ever want or need. Here I am barefooted, holes in both knees of my jeans and as happy as a lark. Now you tell me, what could be better?

Portman Shoals

The Forgotten Settlement

I grew up in the little place called Portman Shoals. Now mostly forgotten, all that's left is

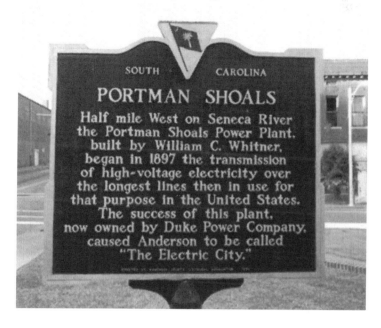

a historical marker pictured above which is located along the roadside on Highway 24 in Anderson, South Carolina. It meant much more to me than that. We were all excited when the talk began of a large lake being built that would back up waters along the Tugaloo and Seneca Rivers. Little did we know that those waters would cover over all our homes and countryside. As beautiful as it is at full pool, a lot of history has been covered and forgotten. In my mind's eye I can still see the old Seneca River Bridge and what was left of the older bridge that once was used to get across the river.

The building above was the office for the Portman Corn Mill.

It sat nestled down by the river making sure there was plenty of cornmeal to go around for everyone. I have tried very hard to get more information on the corn mill and have been told that it was destroyed by fire in the early 1900's. On up above that was the house where the Holden family lived. The Portman Settlement ended right here with Fant's Store. I walked across that bridge many times throwing rocks and sticks into the water just day dreaming, never once thinking I would one day have to leave. I see the river hill that would bottom out at the bridge, a straight stretch of highway that cars and bikers would sometime race down.

Portman Shoals was a small settlement made up of proprietors of four stores and a power plant. This was a close knit group of people that cared about each other. My grandfather and dad owned and operated the J.W. Patterson Grocery Store. The store had a variety of things including groceries, gas and a large inventory of feed and seed for animals. Their store was located on the east side of the Seneca River and was the turnaround point for the Pendleton school district. The families on the west side of the river sent their children to the little town of Townville to school.

The settlement started with Mr. Fant's store on the west side of the river and the other establishments on the east side, being Mr. Palmer's store at the corner of Highway 187 and Highway 24, and the last being what was called back then the "Beer Joint" that opened nights and weekends down closer to the river.

Portman was a unique place with some very special people. My grandfather sold a farm in the Double Springs community and bought all the land he could around the Portman area. At a time, he owned land up one side and down the other on Highway 187 that bordered Interstate I-85. I don't know just how much he owned, but we claimed it all for playing, roaming, hunting and fishing. We knew where all the good fishing holes were as well as spots that would always bring back squirrels and rabbits.

I have talked to a number of family members that lived at Portman and their stories are very similar to what I remember. They too have flashbacks of the good old days that can never be again. I guess Portman to me is like owning my first car which is like the one you see pictured below. It was very special and I remember all the good times that we had in it. I still miss it and it's been gone for a long time.

We had just about anything a person could ever want or need. A nice, quiet, little community with loving and caring people was the heart of Portman Shoals' little village by the river. When you have the best, why would you ever want to leave?

Here I am as a child pictured below, deep in thought, capable of solving all the problems of the world directly from my easy chair...

That is, I knew from the beginning that I was very comfortable and satisfied to stay here for all time.

A Mighty Raging River

We have all heard of the Mighty Mississippi River. I'll tell you it can't hold a candle to the streams that make up the Mighty Savannah River. When Mr. William Church Whitner had the idea of generating power on the Seneca River, he was confronted with a gigantic task. Attempting to harness the power of these mighty waters was an enormous feat indeed. Under normal circumstances and rain conditions, the rivers could reach very high levels. Flooding was a major problem when above average waters would fall. Andersonville, seven miles downstream, was washed away twice and finally moved to higher ground.

The move was about 12 miles east and became known as Anderson, named for General Robert Anderson, a Revolutionary War hero, who came to South Carolina to assist his good friend, Andrew Pickens, in surveying land that had been given previously to the English Colony by area Native Americans. The City was founded in December, 1826 and incorporated by an Act of Legislature in 1833.

The major waters feeding the Savannah River came out of the mountains at an above sea level elevation of over 3500 feet. When waters reached the Portman Shoals Dam, the elevation had fallen almost 2000 feet. In a flood situation with this much drop, heavy rain had the potential to cause tremendous problems.

Portman Shoals Dam and Power Plant had 60+ years of service, but all was not good times. The raging waters flooded it twice and there was

even a time that the entire dam was also washed completely away! It had to be rebuilt and constructed a number of feet higher to help hold the tremendous force of the river. There was also a huge fire that once occurred at the dam as well as an explosion, which destroyed much of the inside.

The efforts of Mr. Whitner at Portman brought technology to a new level and helped advance mankind greatly with an abundant hydro-electric source of energy. I remember hearing conversations when man started their trek of going to the moon that without this exploration, the computer may have never come into being. The accomplishment here would have to fall into the same realm. He was an extremely brilliant young man.

How The Portman Power Plant Came Into Being

The Seneca River had for years been a problem with flooding. This river was fed from mountain streams and all coming down hill. The force of the streams is what was needed to produce power. Anderson and the surrounding areas were very fortunate to have a young man the caliber of William Church Whitner, born in Anderson, South Carolina on September 22, 1864. He graduated from the South Carolina College in Civil Engineering in 1895. He was chief engineer of the Anderson Light and Power

Company, organized December 24, 1894, and began construction of the Portman Power Plant in 1896. The Portman power was turned on November 1st, 1897. The cement used in the construction was imported from Belgium and hauled by wagons to the site. Mr. Whitner figured out how to save costs by not having what is known as stepped-up transformers in order to obtain high voltage. Stanley Electric Company of Pittsfield, Massachusetts, (Subsequently purchased by the General Electric Company) was pioneering in this field and was the only company in America who would wind a generator for 10,000 volts. The company offered to build these generators and Mr. Whitner was advised that these were the first 10-thread, 10,000 volt generators built anywhere in the world for the purpose of this type of commercial use! The late James B. Duke sent his engineers to Portman to witness the experiment. The switchboard was built and equipped with single pole switches with long handles on them like a pitchfork. They were named "Ben Tillman Switches" because of his fame and the nickname was then given him, "Pitchfork Ben". The Stanley Electric

Manufacturing Company stationed a branch office in Anderson in 1896 for the supervision of the building and erecting the electrical plant at Portman. Material was shipped to Pendleton and hauled over the old Portman Road to the construction site. Other branches of Stanley were located in New York, Chicago, Boston, and San Francisco. Mr. William States Lee began work at Portman in 1897 and got his first practical engineering experience under the direction of Mr. Whitner. Mr. Lee went on to become president of the P. & N. Electric Railway System and was Vice President of Duke Power Company until his death. The Plant at Portman was the first long-distance hydroelectric transmission plant built in the United States. The importance of the Portman Plant as being a "first" in this category of electrical development can be regarded in the same relationship as the pioneer aviation at Kill Devil Hill, North Carolina as well as the first Hamburg-Charleston Railway. The Anderson County Historical Society in December, 1956, erected an official South Carolina Highway Historical Marker, but the original marker was covered by waters of Lake Hartwell and another marker, (pictured below,) was erected in May, 1961, which reads as follows:

"1,000 feet due north on a site now covered by Hartwell Reservoir, the Portman Shoals Power Plant, built by William C. Whitner, began in 1897 the transmission of high-voltage electricity over the longest lines then in use for that purpose in the United States. The success of this plant caused Anderson to be called "The Electric City". " Portman Post Office was named for Portman Shoals. J. A. McGill was postmaster. The post office was suspended Saturday, December 15, 1900 until Dr. S. M. Orr secured permission from Washington, D.C. to constitute the Portman Power House as a post office. Letters from Portman went by way of Townville or Broyles to Anderson.

Portman Power Plant helped pioneer the start of modern day technology by providing abundant, stable power from the banks of a small community of river folk. This in turn, electrified the city of Anderson, SC and reached out across our nation and countries beyond. Through the brilliance of a young engineer, William Church Whitner let his light shine throughout the world.

Pictures you see throughout the book are very old and for many the quality is not as good as I would've liked, but many of these images are some of the only remaining pictures that remain, capturing a time long ago now a forgotten memory by most.

The picture above is of the Power Plant with the dam in the distance.

The above picture was taken in the late 1940's or early 1950's.

The next few pages will be pictures of the construction of the Power Plant building. These are pictures that very few people have ever seen and are now over 100 years old.

Above is Highway 24 Bridge from the top of Portman Dam.

The picture above was taken from the new Highway 24 Bridge. If you look slightly to the left in the middle you will see a pier for the I-85 Bridge.

The picture above was taken from the old Highway 24 Bridge.

This picture shows the old and new Highway 24 Bridge with Portman Dam in the distance.

This picture was taken in the late 1930's.

Old Portman Dam was of brick construction and some 68 feet high. The old dam was not removed. The plant itself was gutted and the old crane removed. One of the old power generators is kept on display in Anderson. The dam and powerhouse building now make a good reef for fish. It lies about half way between the Seneca River Bridge on Highway 24 and the I-85 Bridge.

Pictures shown over the next few pages will be of the interior of the Power Plant. They are very rare and I was lucky enough to find a few that were still in good enough condition to view.

These were the first 10,000 thread used anywhere in the world commercially when put into operation at Portman.

Master Control Board

Portman Dam and Power Plant in the early 1900's.

This is the Switch Yard outside the Power Plant.

This is the Switch Yard looking down from the top of the dam.

Anderson's Severest Blow

Wednesday, January 1, 1902

The Power Company's dam at Portman Shoals was swept away and what was once Earle's Bridge was now gone.

At the time, the people of Anderson were confronted with a horrible turn of events when suddenly darkness reigned supreme as the electric current which fueled the entire city was completely shut down. Information soon reached the city that the dam of the Anderson Water, Light and Power Co. at Portman Shoals had washed away! This information was credited by very few at first, but when later it was officially confirmed, it was a terrible shock to the entire citizenship.

The terrible calamity following a disaster of this nature caused a chain reaction of events which left the entire city in a blackout causing thousands of people to be without work. Cotton mills and many other local industries could no longer operate. The streets at night were in total darkness and the private residences were dimly lit by oil lamps and candles.

Portman Shoals Dam was situated nine miles west of the city on the Seneca River. It furnished 3,300 horsepower to Anderson alone and cost over $400,000 to build. The dam was 840 feet long, 44 feet at the highest point and 31 feet 6 inches at the base. This was a major blow to the people affected and to local economies.

The rule for the construction of dams being that the base should be two-thirds of the height, it will be observed that a margin of safety of ten percent had been provided for in the construction of this dam.

The volume of water was so great that 200 feet of the center of this dam of solid concrete had been washed away. It was first thought that the dam was gone entirely to the bottom, but it was later found that ten feet of the base still remained. If the dam's base remained, the coat of repairs would not be so great. Viewing matters in their gloomiest, it was thought that the repairs on the dam would not exceed $35,000.

Almost in an instant after the dam was swept away, the powerhouse was flooded with thirteen feet of water. This house contained all the machinery, and whether this machinery had been ruined was problematical. It was thought it could be dried out and replaced at a nominal cost. If not, and it was ruined, it would entail an additional $50,000, which represented the cost. No very intelligent estimate of the loss could then be made, but in any event, the entire damages would be repaired at once.

The Board of Directors met and as a result of this meeting the Flint Building and Construction Company of Palmer, Massachusetts was telegraphed. They were the largest construction company in the world at the time. They telegraphed back and said that the Superintendent along with an expert would be there by the end of the week. President, Dr. S. M. Orr wrote, "Nothing will be left undone to put matters back in original shape and in this we have the hearty co-operation of all interested in the plant."

The immediate plans of the Anderson Water, Light and Power Co. were outlined by President Orr. An engine would be ordered by telegraph and placed at the Orr Cotton Mills. The boilers of that mill would be powered by this engine and a generator owned by the Anderson Cotton Mills would be moved and set in motion from the energy thus created. In two weeks the city would once again have light and all its minor industries supplied with power. At Portman Shoals an attempt would be made to put in a "false dam" or cofferdam to generate power sufficient enough to run the cotton mills. President Orr thought this could be accomplished in about two months. It may be well to say at this point that since the disaster at Portman the President, Dr. S. M. Orr, had received telegrams of sympathy and offers of assistance from many of the states. His friends at home had been so prompt in expressions of kindness and offers of support that he requested thanks to them, and said that he felt very grateful and would gladly reply to each one personally if his time and health permitted.

So many families that solely depended on their earnings at the mills were thrown out of employment. Two months, two weeks, yes, even two days, meant too much to so many of them that could not afford to be out of work. The mill Presidents were fully aware of this fact and were doing everything in their power as rapidly as possible to relieve these conditions.

The Anderson Cotton Mills were fortunate in being able to furnish power for their 18,000 spindle mill, and they ran night and day, having eight hour shifts, thus giving employment to about two-thirds of their employees. The Orr Cotton Mills were solely dependent on the electric power, but the President had wired for a one thousand horsepower engine and would start the mill just as soon as this engine could be received and placed. Wherever the mill operatives could be used they were given employment, and everything was done for them that could reasonably be expected.

Shortly after the breaking of the dam at Portman, the people were naturally inclined to the opinion that the dam had not been properly constructed. It was rumored that the Electric Water, Light and Power Co. had reserved $30,000 of the contract price until the work was accepted. Also, that the work had not been accepted and that the contractors had instituted suit against the company to recover this unpaid amount. This rumor was investigated and the following found to be the facts: By contract $6,000 of the construction price was to be retained until the work was accepted; that because of minor defects the work had not been accepted, and that the contractors had really filed a mechanics lien to recover the $6,000.

"The conditions at the dam Sunday afternoon show perhaps the greatest flood ever known on Seneca River. At 5 o'clock the water was running five feet deep over the waste-weir. In two hours it rose three feet higher, and continued to rise, running within fifteen inches of the bulkhead. Trees, logs and all kinds of debris were rushing madly over the dam, and at 11 o'clock the crash came."

In the powerhouse were three men Jim Todd, Sam Jackson and Forrest Goggins. Goggins was in charge of the machinery. When the break came and the roaring, hissing and crashing noise told what had happened, Todd and Jackson rushed for the door and escaped. Goggins stopped just long enough to turn off the electric current, but in that moment the water filled the power house to a depth of thirteen feet and Goggins found himself battling in inky darkness against a watery grave, which seemed almost inevitable. Rising to the top and catching a glimpse of a window, he swam to it and made his way through it and on with the rushing current. He landed safely some distance below.

Earle's Grove Bridge three miles below the dam was swept away. This was a steel bridge supported by two huge rock pillars. These pillars were also swept away, which gives some idea of the incredible yet terrible amount of water that came crushing through everything in its path downstream.

The above information was from an article that was published in the first edition of the

Anderson Newspaper following the flooding. It was taken from the South Carolina archives of the Anderson Newspaper. I have been able to locate from the archives of old newspapers and other articles from the early 1900's to factual information passed on in this book. A good bit of what you read in these pages are coming straight from the heart and mind of a young man who loved and cherished our little part of this world.

The Day The Lights Went Out At Portman

December 14, 1913

The story you are about to learn of will be news to most. The event happened almost 100 years ago. This was the day that the Seneca River caught fire. The burning river with flames dancing downstream to the rhythm of the current was a rather feeble anti-climax to the big performance that wintry day.

The sequence of near tragic events began without warning. Operation of the Portman Shoals Power Plant that morning proceeded at a normal pace. The big Stanley generators purred smoothly, producing electricity for the industries and homes of Anderson 10 miles eastward.

Tom Fellers and Junior Harper, the only men on the power house floor, went about their duties in the usual manner, observing machinery and routinely throwing switches. They were having no trouble and anticipated none.

Then abruptly, with the devastating shock of a thunderbolt, chunks of metal flew in all directions. The top half of the armature, weighing tons, crashed through the top of the building, then fell back on the transformers. The picture below was taken December 14, 1923.

Those not shattered were punctured by chunks of metal traveling with the velocity of bullets. A flood of oil gushed upon the floor, and then burst into flames as electric sparks set it afire. To add to the bedlam and terror, the other generators disintegrated with a fiery earth jolting roar.

Junior Harper, his clothes aflame, dashed through the inferno. A jump into the tail race offered the quickest refuge from torment, but Harper couldn't swim a stroke. He ran from the building and plunged into a creek.

As for Fellers, he knew nothing of what was going on. Something hit him on the head and a piece of flying steel split his ankle open. He collapsed under the No. 5 generator and water wheel couplet.

Persons working outside the building rushed to the rescue. They spotted Harper in the creek. Assuming Fellers had plunged into the tailrace, they then ran down the river looking for him, but no trace of him could be found. Meanwhile, fire rampaged through the powerhouse, feeding on the transformer oil. Something had to be done in a hurry.

"FLOOD the power house," somebody cried in a voice shrill with panic. "Raise the fill gates." That was it, a split-second decision. It occurred to no one that four men were down in the penstock, a big round steel case where the water comes in, making repairs on the No. 3 generator water wheel. Here they were safe from the fire, but not from water that might come pouring in.

The gate to the penstock cut the water off completely, but in the big fate was a little gate two feet square called the fill gate. Raise the fill gate and the penstock floods. When this happened that day almost 100 years ago, the four men working on the water wheel were faced with the alternative of staying where they were and drowning or scrambling into the flame filled power house to face the strong possibility of being roasted to death.

No vote was taken. As water began to gush into one end of the penstock, the men went out the other. They met the flames, dashed through them and emerged from the powerhouse without as much as a blister among them. The wet clothes they wore had insulated them against the inferno.

As the flaming oil began to float atop the rising water and drain into the river, a searcher found the unconscious Fellers. The oil fire, which by now had the river in flames for distance of one mile below the powerhouse, missed the prostrate man by less than six feet. Fellers lay unconscious nine days in the Anderson hospital, his skull fractured in two places, back bruised black and ankle gashed. Harper fared equally as bad, if not worse. He had third degree burns over his body. They were both lucky to be alive.

With all the devastation that went on that day, it's a wonder that lives were not lost. Quick thinking on the part of all kept this from happening.

The power plant was out of operation for quite awhile, but due to the fact that there had been outages before because of floods, measures had been taken by the mills in Anderson to make do by generating power for the plants and villages.

Portman Shoals Beach

Not many people know this but we also had a beach at Portman. In the summertime, large sand bars would mound up and sunbathers would come from all around. Those who chose to come on Saturdays could find picnic supplies at the stores around Portman. If you chose to come on Sundays you had to bring your picnic from home as all the stores were closed in reverence of the Lord's Day.

This was a very busy place in the summertime. Sunbathers would come by the droves to lie out in the sun and play in the waters down below the dam. In summers when the water would be down, large sand bars would be left exposed. Several hundred people could be found there on the weekends. This helped the businesses in our little quiet community. The extra people would stop at one of the three stores to get their drinks and picnic supplies. They could do this providing it was before Sunday. As mentioned, all the stores were closed on Sundays in honor of the Sabbath. That's not heard of much this day and time.

As kids, we liked to go and see all the new people that the sand and water brought. We were not accustomed to seeing all those pretty girls in bathing suits. This was a real treat for us. We did have an advantage on newcomers. We knew the terrain and knew where all the good vantage points were and could sit off in the distance and get our eyes full on Sunday afternoon of sunning beauties. We usually had several months in the summer when the weather would be hot and dry and that would keep them coming out and playing in the water and sand.

I can only remember once when there was a problem there at the water. There was a kid from Anderson that got out in the swift water and was pulled under. It took a couple of the adults, but they got him out and after a little while he was alright. He was just scared and embarrassed by the whole thing.

Once the fall rains started, the waters would rise and the sand would be washed away. But with any luck, next year we could start all over again.

I can remember on a number of occasions going up to what was called Sand Island. I'm not sure if it was an island or not but that is what it was called. The location was about three miles upstream in the pond above the dam. I have never seen so much sand in all my life. I can remember it being about 7 or 8 feet high and very white. We would take a picnic lunch and get in our little flat bottomed boat with a very small engine and putter upstream until we arrived. We would play and see what interesting artifacts we could find.

Just like our little beach below the dam, when the big rains would come this too would be washed downstream. A fun time but that too is all gone.

Fourth of July Week at Portman Shoals

This was the most fun week of the whole year. This is the time that the power plant would draw the dam. What this meant was that all the gates would be opened wide to dump all the water from the pond above the dam. This would clean out that area of mud and silt. When this happened, the river below would get muddy and would cause the fish to come to the surface to breathe.

Most would wade the river, but some would brave the waters in boats. This was the time of year that everyone longed for.

Early in the morning on the Saturday that they did this, people would start arriving. The cars would line the roadside from the river hill and on both sides of the bridge and anywhere else they could park. They would come by the car load with their dip nets and sacks to put the fish in.

I was so excited the night before that I would have a hard time going to sleep. I would lay there thinking about all the fun we were going to have the next day. I remember two years in a row after I was old enough to get involved in the event, I woke up with pink eyes. I guess this was the Lord's way of keeping me from drowning. When it came time to go down to the river, I would always get a lecture from my mom about being careful. If you can imagine a twelve year old with a tow sack strapped around his neck in water up past his chest with a dip net trying to catch fish in fast moving water, well that was the situation. It's really a wonder we didn't drown.

A lot of fish were caught each year. The real fun came when we all got back to the house and started cleaning the fish. We would have a big fish fry and all my uncles and their families were there.

This was the highlight of our year. It was a fun time for us. For one thing, we for the most part never saw that many people anywhere other than maybe the county fair when it would come in the fall.

The three stores in our settlement had a banner day in sales of just about everything in the store. People came back from the river wet, thirsty and hungry. I would have to say that it was a fun time for all. I can't ever remember anyone ever getting hurt or any accidents during this time. A memory I will always cherish.

The Old Campground

I remember as a kid I thought the old campground was the coolest place in the whole wide world. The campground was a pretty good trek from the settlement. To get there, you had to follow an

old logging road for almost a mile and cross over a foot log or makeshift bridge when crossing the creek. The logging road was draped over with trees down near the Seneca River. I remember this was one of my favorite places to go. When you arrived there was a widening or clearing and then over to the left you would see a very large old army tent.

As kids we were so fascinated. I remember always being greeted by Mr. John Mundy. He was one of the few black men that called this place home. Mr. John and Grandpa were good friends and Grandpa taught me to never judge a person by the color of his skin. I thought he had about the neatest place I had ever seen. He would take us inside and it was always so tidy. I can still see his cot on one side of the tent. He had a rack where he hung up his clothes and a metal folding table and chairs. Hanging from the center post was his coal oil lantern to light the tent after dark.

Mr. John would always warn us not to go back in the corner. That was where Charlie lived. Charlie was his large black snake. He was there to keep other snakes and mice away. But he also kept me away.

Mr. John worked for Grandpa doing a variety of things. They had a lot of fun joking and picking at each other. Mr. John was also a good cook. The men would catch fish and bring them down to the campground and Mr. John would cook them and they would have a big fish fry. I am told the spirits would also be flowing, if you know what I mean. I now know why the makeshift tables were nailed to trees.

I remember asking Mr. John where he got his drinking water from? He carried me up a ways from the camp to some rocks. In the center were a crack and an indentation. From that came the best water I had ever tasted. Never had I seen anything quite like this. The water came up and was enough there to use and then it would just go back down in the crevasse of the rocks.

I don't know whatever happened to Mr. John. Later on, I went back down there to see him and the tent and all his belongings were gone. I found out from Grandpa that he had gotten sick and I think later on had passed away. He was a real nice man.

The Country Stores

The country stores were unique. Each of them had a specialty. Grandpa and Dad's store was by far the larger of the other two. I enjoyed going to them to see just what they all offered. I remember that Mr. Fant's store had hand-dipped ice cream. I thought it was out of this world. I would walk across the bridge with my nickel and get a nice cone of chocolate ice cream. I can still taste it. He also carried salted mackerel fish. The fish would come to him in a wooden box.

He also carried Gulf Gasoline along with a variety of groceries and a tiny freezer and cooler for meats. I remember the water-cooled Coca-Cola boxes. In those days, you could buy a coke for a nickel. We had a large candy counter. A lot of the candies then were loose and you would go out with a tiny sack full of candy for pennies.

Our store was a distributor for Mobil Gasoline. Back then you didn't just open a station and install pumps and call one of the companies to bring you fuel. You had to be a distributor. I remember hearing my parents tell about when

Highway 24 was redone and widened. The state highway department dropped off a tanker filled with fuel just above the store. Although Grandpa never sold any gas to the state, he was paid a commission on every gallon of fuel they used over the entire project.

We were also distributors for Issaquena Feed and Seed. We stocked feed for cows, hogs, horses, chickens, and anything else that would eat it. Grandpa had purchased the stones to grind corn and was planning to erect a building for a corn mill near the store. He passed away in 1954 and then the talk started about a large lake being built.

The third store in our little settlement was Mr. Dewitt Palmer's store. This store sat on the corner of Highway 187 and Highway 24. It had a variety of items like the other two.

Grandpa's Country Store

My earliest memories would have to be centered on Grandpa and the store. My Grandpa was John Wesley Patterson. My memories are still vivid of the screened doors with the Merita Bread signs embedded into the wire. The old air compressor was to the right and the container that held the loose oil. My job was pumping the oil into the glass bottles with the metal spouts and the screw tops. There was a glider type swing to the left of the front door and old cane bottomed chairs sitting around everywhere. The flying horse for the Mobil gas tanks could be seen outside. Over the years, the gas brands changed. I have seen pictures showing Pure Oil and Standard Oil among other brands.

There was the old hi-test tank that you had to hand-pump the gas up to the glass bottle at the top.   There were two regular tanks and a Kerosene Pump to the left side of the store. There was the grease pit over to the left and the Indian peach tree to the right of it. I thought Grandpa had about the nicest outdoor toilets I had ever seen. They had smooth concrete seats.

Once you got inside the store, the glass candy case was to the left. The above picture is almost identical to the one at the store. Somehow it doesn't look right empty. I can picture all the candy bars and chewing gum and all the penny candy. Yummy! When I was born, I was the only little fellow out there at the time. I am told Grandpa built me a step-up to be able to reach the candy case.

I can picture now the old black telephone that hung on the sidewall. There were telephone numbers written all over the wall. I remember the number to call for a taxi was a three-digit number (108). Their slogan was, "Don't be late, call 108". I also remember the old black adding machine, white scales, wooden saltbox for fatback and the stalk of bananas hanging from the ceiling. I can see the round wood box that had hoop cheese and the large knife that was used to slice it with. Grandpa kept a jar with a slot in the top to put the penny for sales tax. I can see the green shelves with all the groceries and canned goods in them. There was the drink box with the bottles of Coca-Cola and Pepsi, Buffalo Rock Ginger Ale, Toms Orange and Grape, Dr. Pepper and the tiny freezer where they kept ice cream. You could get a 5 or 10 cent cup of ice cream. Popsicles sold for a nickel. Cokes were also a nickel. I can see all the animal feed in the 100 lb cloth print sacks that the women made dresses from. The women were all very good when it came to sewing, cooking or any kind of crafts. My mother was a very good seamstress, but she couldn't hold a candle to my grandmother. I am told that my grandmother would take your measurements, then lay a newspaper in the floor and cut out a pattern for a dress, sew it up and you could wear it home.

There was a large room in the back of the store. On Saturday nights, Dupree Cann and the Lazy River Boys would come and play music. This was a fun time. I remember once there was a guy that came in and did some magic and he could also hypnotize people. He had them saying and doing all kinds of things. The band played mostly country and blue grass music. We heard Lester Flatt and Earle Scruggs tunes as well as Hank Williams. Now if a minister came in the store while the show was going on, the music would change to, "When the Roll is Called Up Yonder".

Dupree Cann (right)

This is my grandmother with all of her children. This was taken in 1955, the year after Grandpa died. Uncle George standing to the right of Grandmother, died in 1960.

This is my Uncle Reece and me. He was the last owner of the store and was the one who closed it down. He and I were the last to leave our little settlement. Uncle Reece never married. He was everyone's friend and all the kids loved him. I think he babysat just about all of us at one time or another.

Family and friends in front of our store

The above picture is of Portman children and
was taken around 1940.

Portman children of parents who worked at the plant

Portman children just having fun

This is a picture of Frank Ray, Felton Thompson (seated), Lonnie Cole and Clint Bolt. All were employees at Portman.

Bream Fishing And The Black Snakes

A typical day for me in the summertime, was rushing up the dirt road to the tailrace to go bream fishing. I had several great fishing spots. I'll never forget one particular summer day when I was around ten or eleven years old. I woke up early and dug my can full of worms and headed out with my cane pole, rigged just right and barefooted. My trek up to the back of the power plant was about a mile up a winding dirt road. I wanted to get there early so I could be sure to get the best fishing spot.

On this particular morning, the sun was bright and there wasn't much breeze in the air. I went as fast as I could, knowing I was going to catch a good mess of fish. No sooner than I had gotten my hook baited and in the water, the cork went under and I had my first catch. I put him on the stringer and tossed it back in again. I was catching one fish after the other. I must have fished for about two hours straight. By this time, I was getting tired and hungry. I had a long stringer full of bream. I have no idea how many, but I know it must have been way over the limit. But to a little kid, this was heaven.

I put the stringer back in the water and reached into my little paper bag to get my peanut butter and jelly sandwich. By now I was about to starve so I wolfed it down and started getting my stuff together to start the trek back home.

I was so proud of my fish. At this time in my life, the size of the fish didn't matter. If it had two eyes, that was good enough for me. I started back to the house with my pole and the stringer full of fish. The stringer was so long that the tails of the fish were touching the ground. I couldn't wait to get back to the store to show off my bounty. As I was walking along, I looked up and just ahead of me in the road was a big black snake. The snake saw me about the same time I saw him. He must have smelled the fish and stopped right in the middle of the road. I froze in my tracks trying to reason out my next move. There was no way I was going to try to get by him on the road. I turned to go back the way I had come from and to my surprise there was another black snake bigger than the one in front, following me. Here I was with a snake to my front and a snake to my rear, a river on one side and a steep bank on the other. I looked back to my front and the first snake had started moving off to the side of the road. Just as soon as his tail got off the road, I began running as fast as I could. I didn't look back for a long way. When I finally did, the snakes were nowhere in sight. I was relieved and out of breath.

When I got back to the store, there were a number of older men sitting around talking. I was out of breath and dragging my stringer full of fish. I tried to tell them about my experience, but I was too out of breath. One of them felt sorry for me and gave me an ice cold Coca-Cola to drink. Man, it tasted good! They kidded me a little about keeping so many small ones, but I cleaned them all and we had fish for supper.

Dad's Encounter With A Snake In The Mud

I remember one spring we had a big rain. The river was out of its banks and was muddy red. Dad said, "Come on, son. We've got to go check the boats to see if they're alright." Just about everybody that lived on the river had a homemade boat of some kind, and he was anxious to check ours out.

We proceeded down to the river. Water was standing everywhere all along the roadside. When we got to the location of our boat, he told me to stay back. He slipped and slid down the sloping bank and emptied the water from inside our boat and the others around it.

We then began to walk the riverbank just to see what we could see. We came upon a really steep bank. Looking down we could see a large water snake making its way across the muddy mess down close to the water. Here is where Dad made his big mistake. He said, "Son, hand me that long stick over there. I am going to whack this snake with it." He had good intentions but when he made a big swing at it he lost his footing and off into the muddy mess he went right in the direction of the snake. I don't know where the snake went. What I do know is that Dad was a muddy mess from head to toe. I tried not to laugh but he sure looked a sight. When he finally got out after several tries, he was not in a good mood and was ready to go home.

I remember another time when Dad and my Uncle Fred were sitting on a big rock out in the middle of Seneca River fishing. They were barefooted and both were wearing overalls with no shirts. Dad asked my uncle if the fish were biting his feet. He replied yes. Dad said, "Mine too." Then he said, "One is trying to get up my pants leg. I'm going to try to catch it." He grabbed his pants leg tight and pulled it out of the water only to find a snake tail hanging out the bottom. I don't know what happened to the snake but that ended fishing for that day.

When they started the long walk back to the store, Dad looked over at my uncle and said, "You know, that didn't scare me a bit." Uncle Fred just laughed and shook his head and said, "Well, at least now your color is back in your face."

Walking The Catwalk On Top Of The Dam

The old Portman dam was 68 feet high and was made of red brick. Up on top of the dam was a flat area and affixed to the top was a board about 8 inches wide. My cousin and I wandered off one morning to see what we could find or get into. We crossed the bridge and looked up toward the dam. I decided we should go up and check it out. From where we were, it could have been about a couple of miles away.

We followed the old road bed as far as we could and then we lit out through the woods. We got to our destination and climbed up the dam. We looked across the dam to the power plant. We inched our way onto the dam moving ever so slow. Then we got out to where we had water on the upper side of us and a long drop down to almost no water and a lot of rocks on the other. This was a sight we had never seen. If I had been there by myself I probably never would have gone out on this thing to begin with, but my cousin had enough dare in him to always get us into trouble. We inched our way out to the first gate with the wheel that the workers would turn to let the water out. We got a little braver and moved out to the next one. By this time, we were in full view of the Seneca River Bridge and could plainly see someone walking across. He stopped and looked in the direction of the dam and started studying the two characters he saw on top. We recognized him about the same time as he did us. It was my uncle and he started yelling for us to get our "you know what's" off the dam. He almost scared us to death but we inched our way back and finally made it back to safety.

The trip back out of there was not nearly as much fun as the trip going. We knew we were going to have the devil to pay when we got home and we were right. By the time we got back, he had already gone and told my dad and we both got our back sides tore up real good.

Other than the Power Plant employees, I guess we were about the only people that had ever walked across the top of the dam. I still don't think the excitement and thrill of that was worth the thrashing we got at home. But it's still a memory and I will cherish it forever.

The Day The Army Came To Portman

One year late in the summer, I was playing outside and I heard the rumbling of vehicles. I looked up and there was a convoy of military vehicles coming down the river hill. I watched intently to see exactly what they were going to do. I could hardly believe my eyes when they pulled off the road and filled the store front parking area and all along the side of the road with their vehicles.

I saw someone in uniform get out of the lead jeep and go over to the store and have a conversation with Dad and Grandpa.

They began emptying their trucks of all their leftover K-rations and piled a stack higher than the store. They then lined up in a single file and a few of them at a time went into the store and made their purchases. I meandered around to get a closer look. One of the soldiers called me over and asked if I could get him a canteen full of hot water. He said he would pay me for it. Boy, this sounded good to me so off I ran to the house with all the canteens I could carry. I filled them and returned. They paid me in change and off I would go again. The water filled canteens got heavy but so did the change that filled my pockets. I saw some of the guys later filling their steel pots with the hot water and they began to shave and wash up. I guess they wanted to look their best for their wives and girlfriends.

This was a very profitable day for Dad and Grandpa at the store as well as for me. Later that day after the army had departed, I went into the store and the shelves were bare. All the soft drinks were gone. The candy was all gone and most of all of the canned goods in the store were gone. I looked over at the small freezer hoping that they had left me a least one ice cream cup, but they too were all gone.

My cousin and I went outside and looked at the mess they had left. I found out later that they had paid Dad a sum of money to allow them to be able to leave their leftover trash from two weeks of camp. We began looking through all the boxes and to our surprise we found all kinds of goodies. We had enough camping supplies for some time to come. You name it, we had it. Hot chocolate, peanut butter, crackers, candy, coffee, can openers and out of all the things we found, we did come across one pack of cigarettes. A wise person would have left them alone, but instead, we got caught smoking, got sick, and then got our pants dusted.

Other than on the fourth of July when the dam was drawn, this was probably the most people I had ever seen at Portman at one time. It looked like Grand Central Station with all the trucks, jeeps, and military vehicles. They were as thick as flies on buttermilk. I remember hearing my parents talk about the power bill being high following this event and Mother complained about not having any hot water to take a bath. I just remained quiet and kept my stash of change hidden. I later told Grandpa about my salesmanship with the military and he just patted me on the head and smiled. I learned a good lesson from the time spent with the military that day. I guess that was my first experience with supply and demand. I still wonder how much money I could have made if I had marketed my wares a little better. I had ice cream and candy money for a long time to come.

There was another time in the history of Portman that the Army showed up. This was immediately after the Japanese bombed Pearl Harbor. The military had reason to believe that Power Plants across the country were also targets of the Japanese forces. The Governor of the State, John Henry Hammond, called out the National Guard to stand guard around the Portman Power Plant. A number of large shells were found at the base of the dam. It was later determined to be from ROTC training exercises from Clemson College (known today as Clemson University).

Telephone Party Line with 14 Families

Back in the day when rural areas were first getting phone service, a private line was not available. I remember that our first phone had 14 people on the line. There was an old saying "children should be seen and not heard". I was told that often about the phone, that it was a device for adults and not children.

I can see my mother now on the phone with her friends and there's no telling how many of them would be on the phone at the same time. This is one way that they could stay caught up on what was happening in the community.

It blows my mind to see all the new fangled phones that are available now. The first phone I remember seeing was the one at Grandpa's store. The phone did not have a dial. To make a call, you picked up the receiver and then hit the switch hook. This would let the operator on the other end know that someone wanted to make a call. You would then either give her (no male operators) a number, which was 3 digits, or you gave her the person's name you wanted to call. Then you would be dispatched through to your party.

If you had an emergency and the line was busy, you just interrupted and told them your need and they would all get off and let you have the line. I'm sure then that your problem got spread all over the community.

Times have really changed. I was speaking to a group of young people at our church and mentioned once having a phone with a party line. The youth Pastor interrupted me and said, "You had better explain party line." Not only did they not know what I was talking about, they had never heard of it either. I also think just about everyone in the room had their own cell phone in their pockets too.

We still hear about the good old days of times gone by. Just look at all the changes that the baby boomers of my era have lived through and witnessed. I have been known to get halfway to church only to realize that I had left my cell phone at home. When this happens, I turn around to go back and get it for fear that I might miss a call. My how times have changed.

Indian Artifacts

The rivers around Portman were all named by Indians. The area earlier was the running grounds of the Cherokee Indians. They lived all

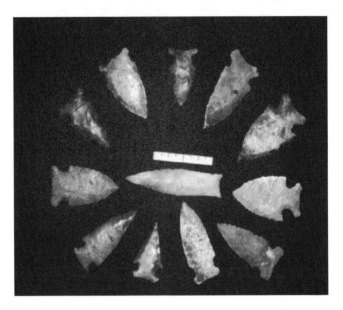

up and down the Seneca, Tugaloo, Three and Twenty, Six and Twenty and Deep Creek. The island directly across from the Portman Shoals Marina had an old Indian Blacksmith Shop on it. We used to find all kinds of relics. I remember one of the families that lived there. Their children would bring pieces of lead to school and use as pencils. The teachers didn't like it much, but the kids thought it was cool.

I still have arrowheads that I found all along the riverbanks while hunting and fishing. As a kid we played all over that area. We went to school with the children that lived there. There was a large ravine on the left side of what now is an island that was deep enough to put several houses in. It now is underwater and should be a good habitat for fish.

I remember on my last visit to Andersonville Island, I looked down in the sand and found one of the largest arrowheads that I believe I have ever found in this part of the country. I think with the right kind of patience, looking around the banks of the lake one could find some nice treasures.

Whiskers The White Billy Goat

Down below the dam there was a large strip of land with trees. On one side was the tailrace with swift water coming down. This was about thirty feet wide. On the other side was all the water coming either through the dam's gates or over the dam in times of heavy rains.

One summer, a large white billy goat came to this area during a time when the water was very low and almost no water at all was coming down. The rains started to come and the water got too deep for him to get off. He claimed the area as his own.

At first he stayed clear of us and we did him. We got more courageous and so did he. We tried to make friends with him but he would have no part of it. He let us know that he meant business and to stay away from him. His temperament let you know that he would get you if the need ever arose.

I remember he had long curved horns and a long white beard. He would chase us and we chased him. We had an ongoing battle with Mr. Whiskers, as we called him. He would see us coming and he sometimes tried to hide from us. Then there were other times when he would chase us with vengeance. I remember once several of us got him by the horns and tried to rub his nose in the sand. That was a big mistake. On occasion I can still feel his horns on my backside where he butted me. It wasn't long before we decided to leave him alone. We named the area "Billy Goat Island".

Moonshine Still

Back in the day, some folks didn't want to pay for store bought whiskey so they would manufacture the hooch themselves. This was illegal and from time to time you would hear about someone getting caught making the stuff.

My story starts here. My cousin and I were about 11 years old at the time. As always we were exploring new areas of the woods. This one day in particular we were in an area that I didn't even know existed. I think it was about two miles from the store. We located a small stream meandering down through a small ravine. Up in front of us, I saw something almost hidden. We both quietly proceeded and to our surprise there it was, the liquor still. I had only seen pictures of them, but here one was for real. My cousin wanted to take a closer look but I stopped him. I was afraid someone might be watching it. There wasn't any activity at the time. We stayed long enough to get our bearing on where it was and the general area around it. Cautiously we slipped back out as quietly as we could and high tailed it back to safer ground.

When we got back to the store we were afraid to talk about it to anyone, for fear that we might be talking to its owner. Later that evening, I mentioned it to my dad and he had a fit. He told me how dangerous it was and that we could have been hurt or killed by whoever it was that owned the thing. He made me promise that we wouldn't go back up there again. That was ok with me. I had all the excitement I wanted for that day.

Spring was here and almost time to start fishing for bream. In the spring we walked the small creeks picking up clumps of leaves and gathering hellgrammites. These were grub like little creatures that made excellent bream bait. They had a tough skin on them and the bream couldn't knock them off.

One day we were having a pretty successful day gathering worms and we saw something kind of shiny in the water. We examined it as we got closer and to our surprise it was a half-gallon jar with clear liquid in it. We opened it and knew right off that it was moonshine, otherwise known as hooch. The more we moved our hands in the sand, the more we found.

Now what do you think two eleven year old kids would do in a situation like this? It smelled too bad for us to drink. We didn't want to burst the jars. So we decided to take it all and hide it somewhere else. We did just that and then went about our business just like nothing had ever happened. This little game of hide and go seek had gone on for a day or so when my dad called me in. He said he had something he wanted to discuss with me. I knew I must've done something wrong, I just wasn't sure what he had caught me doing. He asked me whether or not I had found any jars. I must have given him the "deer caught in the headlights look" because he said, "Ok, where is it?" I told him where we had hidden it and that we didn't drink or break any of it. He just shook his head and walked off. I found out later that the moonshiners had the stuff hidden all around our property. Later, we went back to our hiding place and it was all gone. I never found out who it belonged to. Maybe it belonged to kinfolk or maybe a stranger, but that was my last time to mess with somebody else's hooch.

I was out on the backside of Grandpa's house one day. I saw all these churns in a row with cloth tied around the top and they smelled strong. I asked my dad what was in them and he said that Grandpa was making some medicine. I found out later that it was homemade blackberry wine. Grandpa died and I guess my dad finished making the wine. I know for a long time we had a large jar of it at our house. In fact, to this day I still have what is left of that wine in a small jar at our house. It is probably about 60 years old.

Sunday Afternoon In Baker's Pasture

Every Sunday afternoon all of the kids would get together and head for Baker's pasture. I don't know if I ever met Mr. Baker, but he had a rather large rustic house on the river that he rented out. At the time, one of my uncles and his family lived there. Just below the house about a half-mile away was a large pasture where he grazed a large herd of white-faced Hereford cows. The pasture was nice and flat and made an ideal place for a bunch of kids to spend an afternoon playing baseball.

We would choose up sides and put rocks down for the bases and let the game begin. When we started playing there, at first the cows were inquisitive and would come up to see what was going on. Maybe they thought we brought them food. They soon just ignored us. The only problem with playing there was watching out for all the presents they would leave behind. When we played baseball, you just didn't want to step or slide into something. The smell lasted a long time, and it was one that you would not soon forget.

We played there all afternoon until it was time to go back home and get ready for church that evening. I was brought up in a family that if the doors of the church were opened then you had a need to be there. We were there early and usually stayed late.

Today if you are heading east on Highway 24 and are at the Seneca River Bridge, Baker's pasture would've been to your immediate right. Like everything else, it is under water also. I think Mr. Baker must have owned several hundred acres along the west side of the river. We had a lot of fun times there.

Indoor Plumbing

Indoor plumbing, that's a term that you almost never hear now. But back in the day, in the late 1940's and early 1950's you saw mostly outdoor toilets set back away from the house.

When Dad built our house in the late 1930's we had a bathroom in the house. It was called that but there was nothing in it. It was just a room that he and Mother had plans at some time in the future to put one in. Until then we had to make the trek out to the back of the yard to the little outhouse with two holes and a make shift door on the front. I don't know why most of them had a place for two people to sit. I can't imagine plopping down beside someone to do my morning's business.   Going out to the outhouse in the morning wasn't all that bad but having to go at just about dark for a little fellow was holy terror. I would go with a flashlight in one hand running just as fast as I could say the 23rd Psalm. I had it timed to where when I left our back steps I was saying, "The Lord is My Shepherd" and by the time I hit the door of the outhouse I was at "I will dwell in the House of the Lord forever". I would do the same thing going back to the house. I suppose it was a good way to learn Bible scriptures.

The day came when some large boxes were delivered to our house and were moved into the "bathroom". Dad uncrated them and put everything in its place.

This was about the prettiest thing I had ever seen. The big bathtub had claw feet and ivory knobs. Little did I know all of the work that went into putting it all into operation.

When I got home from school one Friday, I noticed a large pile of cement blocks, sand and cement mix sitting in the yard. Dad didn't work on Saturdays so on that day we got out of bed early and worked long. I didn't know I could be so sore. We dug the hole for the septic tank and the drain line. This was not done all in one day. Over a period of time we got it all in place and covered it up and got the grass planted back. I felt pretty good about what we had accomplished, but still had no idea how it was all going to work.

As I mentioned, indoor plumbing back then was rare. I remember our neighbors and customers coming into the store being very inquisitive about what we were doing at our house. One person in particular wanted to know if we were digging a storm shelter or a fruit cellar. Others wanted to come over just to see it flush. We had several firsts in that house. I saw my first television program and had my first flush.

The day finally came when the job was finished. We had hot and cold running water in the bathroom. Dad called me in and told me to pull the lever on the commode. I got to do the first flush. I felt so important. It worked. At that time, I think we were the only family in our little community that had a real honest to goodness bathroom with indoor plumbing and we had done it all ourselves.

Outdoor Toilets

As I said, most people back then did not have indoor bathrooms. Most used outhouses. It was amazing to see the different types of little houses people built. We have all seen the one with the moon crest in the door. The thing that amazed me the most was the seating. Most always they would have two places cut out for a person to sit. They were usually pretty rustic too. Some were cut smooth and rounded somewhat. But for the most part, there was a diamond shaped hole in the center of a piece of the plank for the seat. The smell was never good and you had to be on the lookout for critters such as wasps, bumble bees, hornets, snakes, spiders and the like. I remember an older man who lived below us that went out one morning to his outhouse, dropped his overalls, sat down, and picked up the latest Sears Roebuck catalog for some reading. A hornet got him from underneath! He came running out of his outhouse hollering and carrying on with his overalls down around his ankles. Now, that was a site to behold. After that, I always checked the best I could to make sure I was the only thing in there before I sat down.

Grandpa had the nicest outdoor toilet I've ever seen. He had concrete floors in it and it had a smooth concrete slab with a well planned out seat in the center. The only problem I ever encountered with it was when I had to go in the winter. The seats were very cold and would get your attention when you sat down.

Dead Man's Curve

Not many folks today remember "Dead Man's Curve". This was an area near the Portman Shoals Marina. If you are on the Double Bridges looking toward the marina downstream you would be looking over what was then known as Deep Creek. On the east side of the lake in this same area was the Green Pond landing. The old road was very winding with a very sharp curve. There were a number of wrecks along there and the road led down to a one lane concrete bridge.

This area was prone to flooding and I can remember several times when the bridge was completely covered. When the lake was built, this bridge was left and is now covered with water. A new bridge was built below what is now the Twin Bridges and I believe it too was covered at least once from flood waters or at least traffic was stopped until the waters went back down. Before the lake was built, I have seen waters almost up to where Highways 187 and 24 crossed. Before the lake backed up, Highway 24 came through the center of all the boat slips at Portman Shoals Marina and Highway 187 intersected with it there.

The area around Dead Man's Curve was a spooky place at night, especially on a foggy, rainy night. Back then we didn't have all the brightly colored lines on the highway or the shiny centerpieces as we have today. If it was foggy, you just about had to feel your way through there. The bridge was just wide enough for a single car to get across. I mean, it was really narrow. I was always afraid we were going to run off into the water.

Gilmer's Camp

I never met Mr. Waymon Gilmer who owned the property up behind the dam on the west side of the Seneca River. There was a very large red brick building with large fireplaces in each end. This was used for Boy Scout jamborees. In addition to the building, there was at one time a spring fed lake and a number of cabins nestled back in the woods. This was a popular place in the summertime for all kinds of activities. I am told that Anderson Boys High School would come out there for their Football camp during summer break.

There were a number of small cabins scattered around the pond. Most of them were painted or stained a dark color. I think some of the coaches stayed in them while the players would hunker down in the large brick building. Since all of the toilets were outdoors, the boys would bathe in the spring fed pond. The pond came about after the dam was built. Mr. Whitner had the rock mined from the area that was used in building the powerhouse. This left a pretty good space and some springs came up from their blasting.

I remember once after we moved away from Portman and before the water backed up, I went there with my Scout Troop from our church. I was one of the older Scouts so I helped our Scout leader try and keep all of the smaller ones in line. We built a fire in the fireplace and got our lanterns going to help light up the place after dark. I got them all bedded down. Somehow a man from Anderson found us and told my Scout leader that his wife was getting ready to have her baby so he left me in charge of the troop and headed out.

This was a shocker and although I was familiar with the area, I had not intended to be there with all those little kids by myself. This was in the day before cell phones and not a lot of people even had telephones. I managed to get us through the night and fixed us some breakfast the next morning. Later we broke camp and started the march back over to the old store.

The Scouts kept wanting to know where the Scout Master was and what happened to him and how were we going to get back to Anderson. He had originally left his car over at the old store and we then hiked about 2 miles up to the campground. When we got to the store the car was gone. I went in to talk to my uncle and he let me use the telephone to try to get help. He called the Boy Scout Troop in and treated them all with ice cream. We were finally rescued and carried home. I heard later that the Scout Master got into trouble with the parents for leaving us all there overnight. But it all ended well, Boy Scout motto "Be Prepared".

Times were changing fast and people were more mobile and the camp I guess lost some of its uniqueness. On several occasions the cabins were broken into and vandalized. Mr. Gilmer talked to our friend Mr. Evan "Ev" Williams about tearing down the cabins and building them a house to live in. He said, "I know you are a good carpenter and there is plenty enough lumber to make a good sized house and you can live in for free as long as you desire." He agreed and that's what happened to the camp and all of the cabins. I know this to be true because it came from my lifelong friend, Mrs. Lois Williams Gleason.

The Williams clan is pictured below. They lived just across the bridge.

Altar In The Woods

While gathering information on Portman, James "Jimmy" Cole asked me if I remembered my altar in the woods and the white cross. That caught me a little off guard. I remembered, but I couldn't recall him ever knowing that I had one. We talked a bit about it and I told him that I did take the cross with me when I finally left Portman.

My altar in the woods was a place that I cherished dearly. It was a special place where I could steal away, a place of quietness, and a place I held very dear. I miss it still today.

I had a dear family friend, Mr. Joe Gambrell, who made the small cross for me when he heard that I had an altar in the woods. I would go there just to get away from everything. In this busy world we live in today not many take the time to get away to themselves and meditate, pray and think things out. I always took a small rock with me when I went there and they piled up as time went on. I was raised in a Christian family. We went to church at least three times a week. We went early and stayed late. I still contend that everyone needs a quiet place that they can go and pray and sort things out.

Now, 50 plus years later I still go to my quiet place in the woods. I have my little altar with a pile of rocks to remind me of previous times that I have used this place to think things through. Occasionally, I have taken my grandchildren there. It gives me a thrill when one of them asks Poppa to take them back to his special place. I want them to learn that their Poppa puts value and worth in getting off by oneself and having quiet time. I had parents who loved me along with neighbors and friends who watched over and cared for me.

Portman Shoals – A Special Time

I don't know if any of us realized until it was all gone just how special our little part of the world was. Here in this corner of the upstate lived a group of people who were closely knitted together and genuinely concerned and cared for each other.

Springtime would find just about everyone getting their garden spot ready for planting. We always had a big garden. My parents planted an ample supply of just about everything that would grow. I remember that cutting okra got to be my job because it made my mother itch. My dad bought a home canner and set it on the back porch. When tomatoes, beans, peas, corn and the like starting getting ready, they would start canning. This gave us good food to eat all winter. We always had enough to share with neighbors and kinfolk.

I remember Grandpa once had an old cow that had gone dry, meaning she stopped giving milk. He decided to slaughter her and cut the meat up and make beef stew. He was kidded a bit but he went ahead with his project. He cooked the meat in a large black pot, seasoned it just right and then borrowed Dad's canning equipment and put all the beef stew away. When winter came he opened up several cans and man alive, we all ate our fill. Grandpa was good at just about everything he did and we now knew he was also a very good cook.

Getting back to the home gardens, Grandpa also grew a lot of things to sell at the store. He would plant several acres of watermelons, cantaloupes and sweet potatoes. I can just hear him now saying, "Bucky (my nickname), go pull us a couple of the smaller melons and put them in the shade for later today." I always enjoyed going with him and we would slip away to our hiding place and burst a cool melon and munch away.

Grandpa with family

Sunday afternoon on the front porch

When late summer would come, the women folk of the community would all come together at the store and go to the room that Grandpa had built on the side of the store and gather around a quilting frame hanging from the ceiling.

I can still see the quilting frame hanging from the ceiling and all the women around it talking and quilting. I guess this was a way of keeping us all warm in the winter and a time to catch up on all that was going on in the community.

They would quilt until all had an ample supply of warm bedding for the cold winter coming up. They made just about every kind of quilt but I do remember a lot of patchwork quilts. To some reading these pages this would seem foreign. Nowadays, when we get chilly we just go turn up the thermostat, but not back in the day. Some heated with coal with a coal grate in an open fireplace. Some heated with wood with a wood stove and a few had individual oil heaters. The nights would still get very cold. I can remember many times going to bed with a hot water bottle at my feet or a brick that had been heated by the fire and wrapped in a towel. That was good for awhile, but then over in the morning your foot would push up against what was then a very cold chunk in the bed. Winters were cold and houses not nearly as warm back then as they are now. But we survived, and I would not take anything for the experience. I think back then neighbors were just closer and I guess for the fact that we all had to depend on each other it made us close. Yes, Portman was a very special place in history and in my mind forever.

My Uncle Willie Patterson was the inventor in our family. He had a number of patents to his credit. He was always making or building something. He built a number of the houses in our settlement. I remember he went down to the branch and built a frame, dredged sand, and made cement blocks. He used steel oil cans in the center to make the blocks light. He built two houses with his homemade blocks. He was a very smart man who taught me to do lots of things.

This is Dad (left) and Uncle Willie (right) in front of the house he built on the lake in Hartwell, Georgia. This house had several stories. The top floor was a small bedroom. He had the bed fixed on wheels with a pivot on one end so the bed could be facing several different vantage points on the water. He also cut out paper silhouettes of a man sitting in a rocking chair with a shotgun in his lap. These were placed in front of the windows and a small lamp would come on at night. This gave the appearance of someone on night watch at the house. I don't think he ever had a problem with any prowlers.

Portman Power Plant Bows To Progress

Like a good captain, L. F. Lon Cole, superintendent of the Portman Shoals Power Plant in Anderson County, is "going down with his ship".

December 9, 1960 at midnight, the switch was pulled to silence forever the historic plant on Seneca River. This river had supplied the power to run the turbines and generators since 1896. For 43 years Lon Cole had had a hand in the operation of the plant and while he could have retired several years earlier, he insisted that he be allowed to remain until the plant was no more.

Mr. Cole's home during a winter snow.

In 1923 Cole helped install the No. 4 Generator at Portman. He pulled the switch, which started the generator into operation. Each night at midnight, his youngest son, James, was the man on duty that pulled the switch to stop the operation.

A crew moved in to begin dismantling the plant and salvaging whatever possible for sale as junk. The work took about six weeks, ending just about the time the waters of mammoth Hartwell Reservoir began backing up from the dam about 14 miles downriver. When this was all completed, Cole would begin his retirement.

A nearby hill was where Cole lived. By this time, that home along with all other structures in the nearby area had been removed.

The above picture is Mr. Lon Cole, the last superintendent of the Portman Shoals Power Plant.

Cole and his wife came to this location shortly after their marriage. During their years there, they raised five children and have seen them all married. Cole upon leaving Portman moved back to his native Townville. He said he was ready to spend time with their nine grandchildren and six great grandchildren. In remarks to the local newspaper, Cole said he recognized that change had to come. When he came to Portman it produced electricity for all of Anderson and that included the streetcars. At the end of Portman's history it only supplied power for the Townville area. Portman had been a big part of his life. When asked what he thought about Portman coming to an end, he said, "Well, I am still fretting over the fact that there are no more steam locomotives."

This marked the end of an era that had brought much advancement to the area and set the region, state, nation and world on a surefooted path to progress.

Through the years, a number of men worked at the plant for Mr. Cole. I have tried diligently to get all of their names. I am listing below the ones that I was able to locate. First, I will list the names of the men who worked and lived at the plant site with their families.

Walter Hill   Sam Jackson

Jimmy Cole   John Hatcher

Lonnie Cole   Frank Ray

Felton Thompson   Clint Bolt

A number of others that lived in the immediate area and worked there include the following:

Evan Williams

Dan Shirley

Joe Gambrell

Tom Hunt

Manel Davis

Furman Thrasher

Larry Palmer

Edgar Breazeale

A Sad Time At Portman Shoals

I guess we all have had some sad times in our lives. My childhood was super. I had lots of friends and we played and roamed all over the Portman area. Probably the fondest memories I have all include my Grandfather, Grandpa as we called him. If you get right down to it, he taught me just about everything I know how to do. It's not that my dad wasn't there for me it's just that Grandpa was more available. Grandpa taught me to fish, hunt and work. Yes, it was not all fun and games with him, but he made it very interesting. I always liked spending time with him. He always made me feel special and was interested in what I wanted to do.

I remember my first hunting experience with Grandpa. I kept looking for his gun as we walked to the woods. We got to the spot he wanted to hunt in and he instructed me to clear out a large place so we wouldn't be making any noise. We sat down and he took a small caliber pistol out of his coat pocket and loaded it. I thought that surely he would have hunted with a shotgun or rifle. He instructed me to be quiet and to sit very still. We sat for a little while and with his eyes he directed me to a spot on the tree where a squirrel was playing. Slowly and quietly he positioned himself so that his hand would be steady. I waited and waited for what seemed like forever for him to shoot. Finally, he fired and the squirrel hit the ground. Grandpa told me to go pick up the squirrel and bring it back. I did and to my surprise he had hit it right in the head. I found out real quick what an excellent marksman he was. We would set up coke bottle caps on a dirt bank behind the store and Grandpa would step off about 30 paces and with his Colt 38 Special he would shoot the center out of them. He was quite a man.

In addition to teaching me to do many things, Grandpa also taught me not to just hunt but how to clean and prepare whatever we brought home. When I got older, I knew how to dress rabbits, squirrels, turtles and the like. He taught me the value of doing a job right, not to just get by, but to do it right. He put a lot of value in being worthy for our keep, as he put it. He said we were to be good stewards of what we were blessed with and to never take it for granted.

Grandpa also instilled in me a love for selling and I made a career out of doing just that. My first job was shining shoes at the store for ten cents a pair. My next job was selling candy at school. I would take a box of Baby Ruth candy bars and sell them for ten cents each.

If the truth is known, I thought that the sun rose and set wherever Grandpa was. As I got older, I knew that someday he would no longer be around. I just hoped that day would never come.

I remember Grandpa having occasional dizzy spells and he would have to sit down or hold onto something at times. One morning he called me and asked me to come to his house and stay with him for awhile. I was 12 years old at the time. I could tell that everything was not just right.

The morning was warm and we sat on a bench outside. I began to ask him questions about how he felt. He said that he would be alright but that he just didn't want to be by himself. I tried to get him to let me call someone for help, but he said no. Finally whatever was happening eased off and he began to stir around so I went home.

When I got back home, I ran in the door and told my parents about what had happened. I'm not sure as to what all happened after that, but Grandpa ended up in the hospital. He got permission from the doctors for the kids to come and see him. I, along with a few of my cousins, went to the hospital to see him. He tried to put up a good front, but I could see in his eyes that he was a sick man. We hugged him and went back home. In a few days we got the news that he had passed away. This was the saddest day of my life. I really thought the sun had risen and set for the last time.

My grandparents were married almost 56 years when he died. Grandpa died in June of 1954. My grandmother died at the age of 89 in 1972.

I didn't want to go to Grandpa's funeral. I guess you could say I was in denial. I was hoping it was all just a very bad dream. It has been said that all good things must come to an end. For me, this certainly was true.

As I grew older, I could see Grandpa in the way I did things. I could see him in the way I would reason things out. Every time I picked up a hammer or saw I thought about him. Even today when I go hunting or fishing, I feel like he is right there with me.

I thought his death was bad, but when it came down to leaving Portman Shoals, the country store, our house and all the places I held dear, that was another thing. The time drew near when we would all have to leave.

After Grandpa's death, my dad sold his part of the store to one of my uncles. The Corps of Engineers sent people around to tell property owners what they would pay them for their homes and land. You were also given the opportunity to purchase back from them the salvage rights to your home. Dad bought our house back and then resold it. He and my mother purchased property in Anderson and built a new home there. The house was brick, nice and all brand new throughout. But somehow, it just wasn't home to me.

I talked to my uncle who purchased the old store about living with him until the store had to be closed. He agreed so I finished out the school year living with him. At least I could still see all the places I had loved for so long.

This was my life. I was there when the house moving company came and jacked up our house and moved it off of what had been our property for many years. The place looked so lonely and empty with it gone. I would go and sit on the brick steps, which were all that was left.

Finally, the old store building was all that was left, as one by one all the other houses were moved and gone.

Evan "Ev" Williams' home being moved and set up at a new location.

This is the Williams' home being moved across old Seneca River Bridge.

This was the home being moved. Mr. Evan Williams' daughter Lois and her husband Hugh Gleason made this their home until his passing several years ago. Lois still enjoys country living there today.

This is Mrs. Emmy Williams standing on the west side of Seneca River Bridge with our little settlement in the background.

Mr. Evan "Ev" Williams taking a bike ride

In the background of the above picture, you can see the house my dad built in 1939. I remember Dad telling me that when the Highway 24 Bridge was being built, he noticed some very large pieces of lumber that appeared to him would be thrown away. He talked to the person in charge and he was told they planned to just drop them off into the water. Dad then asked if he could tie them off and have them. He got the okay and they soon became the sills for our house. I am told that for a single story house back then, this lumber would be 2"x10". The sills for our house were 8"x12". The moving company said that our house moved very well.

Our little Garden of Eden soon became a ghost town. The day the old store building was moved was the final nail in the coffin. I moved on into Anderson with my parents and tried to make a new life for myself. It wasn't all bad but it wasn't Portman and it never really felt like home to me. In my mind's eye, even today more than 50 years later, I can still see all the places I held dear and still do and will until I am no longer here.

Seneca River with lake water backing up

Piers for Highway 24 Bridge

This view is from above the old Portman dam. The new Highway 24 Bridge can be seen in the distance. This gives you a good idea of how deep the water is there now. The I-85 Bridge would be about the same distance to the rear of this vantage point. At the time it was built, the Highway 24 Bridge was the tallest of its kind in the United States.

Andersonville Island

Andersonville Island, the largest island on the lake has a lot of history. At one time, this was a thriving little section of the upstate. The river was used to float cotton goods from the mills in the upstate to the Savannah Port in Savannah, Georgia. Barge like boats were used to transport the merchandise.

The town leaders had hoped for the railroad to come through Andersonville, but because of the threat of floods and the flooding that had occurred, it was bypassed. After the railroad bypassed Andersonville, the settlement moved a few miles closer in and its name was changed to Anderson as it still is today.

Some of our family had a small cabin on the Tugaloo River at Andersonville. We spent time there in the summer.

Dad fishing at the cabin on Tugaloo River

Watermelon time at Tugaloo River with Grandpa and family

A ferry would carry you into Hartwell, Georgia. This was also where the barge would run to and from Savannah, Georgia. The ferry service ceased when a bridge was built over the Savannah River.

The picture below is of the ferry at Andersonville. This picture dates back to 1939. Notice on the ferry, are two Model T Ford cars as well as people.

When the land was bought, the chore of moving graves came into being. The little Andersonville Baptist Church was there and the congregation built another church closer to Anderson, but still near the lake. Their graves were moved and also a number of unmarked graves were moved. Records show that graves were moved to a number of different churches in the area. I also believe that Indian and slave graves were moved.

I remember as a kid running up and down the hills of Andersonville and seeing markings on rocks. Some were legible and we knew them to be graves. I bet if you looked today, you could still find some of the old graves that were never moved.

Andersonville was kind of a throw back in time. It was almost a little ghost town. As kids, we thought it was neat. The pavement ran out just before you got there, and we liked to run in the dirt barefooted. At one time, Andersonville was a very busy place with a number of stores, a mill and a clock factory. If I remember correctly, there was also some kind of school for girls. Flooding washed the mill away once. It was built back, but then flooded again. By the time I came along, the only thing left was a country store. I remember the building was unpainted both inside and out. Gone and forgotten by most, but still a vivid memory.

I remember once in the summer we were playing along the river and saw a number of canoes coming downstream. They were all dressed in their Boy Scout uniforms. There was one spot in the river that was very swift. Each of the canoes followed the same path and when they got to this one spot they would turn over. We thought it was funny and began to laugh at them. They didn't appreciate our laughter and proceeded to tell us. The scoutmaster separated us and suggested that we settle our differences with boxing gloves. I felt pretty good with that idea, at least at first. I could usually hold my own, but had never once had on boxing gloves. It became very apparent that the boy in front of me had. It didn't take me long to find out I didn't like boxing. We shook hands after it was all over with and we wished them well as they went on their way. I think we still had the last laugh. We knew the river better than they did and the rapids on downstream were much worse than what they had come down.

Andersonville Island today has a large deer population and a number of other animals. Now when the waters are down, you could probably still find Indian artifacts all along the shores of the island as well as other interesting things of days past.

For years, there has been talk of making a development of some kind on the island. I remember once a golf course was mentioned. I think there was also serious talk of putting a lake resort on the island and either ferrying everyone out there or building a bridge.

A beautiful part of the lake is taking a boat ride up the Tugaloo River. Most of it is narrow and winding. We had a cabin in the Reed Creek area of the lake on the Georgia side. We would take our boat and go by water to the marina there to get fuel. I remember once on one of our trips for fuel, I looked up several bends ahead of us and coming down the middle of the stream was a Ford truck with a camper on the back of it. I did a retake because from a distance it appeared to be floating down the river. As it got closer, I saw it was a barge and the truck was strapped to it. They pulled into the shore, tied up and made camp for the day. I think if I was a drinking man, seeing that thing coming down the middle of the stream probably would have been very sobering. If you have never been up that side of the lake, you owe it to yourself to take an afternoon and follow the stream up past I-85 to see the pretty sites along the shores.

Our First Boat

I can remember our first boat. A bat toe is a flat-bottomed boat with narrow gunnels or sides.

We had several over the years and all were handmade. The idea to make them float was to fill them full of water and let them sit for a day or so to let the wood swell. If not, you would sink in a hurry. The boats were about 12 to 14 feet in length and would move quickly in the water. Boats of this kind were about all you saw along the river. We would tie them up along the riverbank and come back later to use them again. I can't ever remember finding one locked. Back then everyone was very trusting and had no need to be otherwise. I remember one older gentleman who moved up from Florida and he too had a boat very similar to ours. On the back of his was an attachment that sat above the water with what appeared to be a fan blade. To us, this was about the weirdest thing we had ever seen. In fact, when my younger cousin saw it for the first time he came running to me to tell me about a guy he saw with an airplane on the water. We found out later this was what they used in the everglades in Florida where the water was shallow. At that time he had the fastest thing on the river.

We never had a boat other than the ones we built until the lake backed up. Dad found someone with a 15' wooden boat with a 35 horsepower Johnson motor. He bought it and we found out very quickly that it leaked. We carried it and had it fiber glassed. This added weight to an already heavy boat. I taped it out and striped it like it was on fire. I painted it a fire engine red and you could see me coming from a long way off. We kept that boat for several years and then Dad broke down and bought us a new fiberglass runabout and had our motor installed on it. We thought we were hot stuff. The new boat would fly since it was so much lighter than the other one. This shiny new boat opened up some new avenues for me. I was a young man with girls on my mind and they liked the water and the sun. We had some fun times.

One of my uncles was a good craftsman. He was a person who was always building something. He decided he wanted to build a cabin cruiser. He worked and worked for weeks on the construction. I mean, it was a sight to behold. He thought he had done everything to make it watertight.

After the finishing touches, he decided it needed a good paint job so he dressed it out real good. The day came to launch "The Queen Dorothy". They loaded it up and headed for deep water. They launched the boat and started across the channel. About halfway across, she started taking water and to the bottom she went. They swam back to shore and watched the swell and the bubbles it made. His plans for building boats for others went down like the Titanic. That was the last of the big boat building for our family.

My First Experience Skiing

My love for fishing was still there, but the call for skiing was loud and most of my friends could already ski. One Sunday afternoon, a couple of friends and I went to the lake. We stopped at Big Bass Valley, a store at waters edge just off of old Highway 24, and I purchased a ski belt, ski rope and a pair of skis. That day I was going to become Ski King. The water was white capping and rough. I dropped one of my buddies off into the water with the new skis and threw him the rope. He pulled right up and was going from one side of the boat's wake to the other. I thought, "This looks easy. If he can do it, I know I can." Well it was finally my turn, so into the water I went. I thought I was going to drown just getting the skis on. Finally I was ready to be pulled up. I came up and went straight back down. This went on for a while and finally I made it up. I guess I looked like a kid taking his first steps or riding a bicycle for the first time. I was jerky and then it happened. I got brave enough to leave the pattern of the boat and venture out. Then, a wave caught me. I didn't know water could hurt so much. I had had enough for my first time. Getting back into the boat was another thing. By this time, I was so tired I could hardly get in. Finally I made it back in and we all high fived each other of my accomplishment. When I woke up the next morning, I was sore in places I didn't know could get sore and the following day was even worse. I finally got up enough courage to try it again. The water was like glass and I mastered the sport and then graduated to slalom skiing. We had many wonderful days on the lake skiing and enjoying the lake at its best.

Skiing With Dad

Skiing with dad was another story. When both of us wanted to use the boat at the same time, I would have to compromise. Dad was willing to let me go along and ski if I wanted to, but only on his conditions.

The conditions were if he saw someone or something that he wanted to spend some time with, that is where we would stop. Then, there was the chore of swimming with skis back to the boat when he would stop without warning. The worst of that scenario is when I would get let down in treetops, since the lake was still in the filling process. I found out real quick that the treetops were infested with all kinds of land critters just waiting for a way back to dry land. But all in all we had some fun times together. Now that he is gone, I would give anything to have the opportunity to spend more time with him on any terms.

Effects The Lake Had On The Entire Area

When the talk first started about a large lake being built no one had a clue as to what all it would end up affecting. To start, businesses would have to be relocated either directly from the water or because the community they served would now be on a dead end road that ended up in the lake. Churches had to be moved for the same reason. Miles and miles of roads had to be rerouted because of the water. School districts were changed because of the now new boundaries. A number of bridges were either covered by water and left or were salvaged for the steel that could be taken from them. A number of roads still have their old names with Ford or Ferry on the end of them and in a number of locations parks or boat ramps have been built.

The creation of Lake Hartwell created life style changes for residents living in both South Carolina and Georgia. A number of counties in both states were affected. If you drive around today on rural country roads you will find that some end at the water's edge. In some cases businesses were expanded due to their location and the type of business that it was. In other cases they were relocated or closed.

The up side to all of this, new businesses were founded. The water created a need for water craft, supplies and boat docks. Homes started going up in areas that in times past were either totally deserted or farm land. The lake caused a boom to both South Carolina and Georgia in recreational equipment and housing. The lake properties still have the fastest growing and quickest increase in value.

The lake took away my homeland, but made a very large playground for thousands of people. Mr. Whitner started it with his brilliance of creating and sending power over miles of power lines. I wonder if he ever thought it could all end up like it has?

Historical Pictures of Portman Shoals

PORTMAN POWER PLANT, SENECA RIVER, ANDERSON, S. C.

This is a postcard depicting the Portman Dam and Power Plant and its location.

DOES IT SEEM SO LONG AGO?

The Portman power house is now under water due to the impounding of water for the Hartwell Reservoir, but it has been in the drink before. On August 16, 1928, flood waters swirling down the Seneca drowned out the power house.

This picture is from the Anderson Independent Mail. The Power Plant by this time had been shut down. The waters on the left are back waters of Lake Hartwell now backing up on the old dam.

This picture was taken around 1902 after a big rain.

This was taken from the new bridge in the fall of 1960.

This is the generator from the old Portman Power Plant being taken to Anderson to be put on display. This was the end of an era. At the time the Power Plant was built it seemed huge, now dwarfed by the enormity of the Hartwell Lake.

This picture is of Portman Power Plant back in the 1930's.

This is the Savannah River from the Louie Morris Bridge Highway 29 into Hartwell, GA. This view is looking downstream below Hartwell Dam.

Louie Morris Bridge with Hartwell Dam in the background

The Image In The Mirror

When but a boy, heroes I had many.
Gazing in the mirror I was all of them...Roy, Gene,
John, Wild Bill and Wyatt all tied into one.
The bad guys were no match for my lightning fast
draw and six-shooter gun!
Little boys have heroes, big boys have dreams while
staring in the mirror.
I became one of sports' all-time greats with Johnny,
Joe and Kenny. We knocked the cover off many a
baseball with the likes of Babe, Hank and Mickey.
Big boy's thoughts and dreams turn to girls and
Wow how things change!
There was Marilyn, Betty, Jane and Liz.
They kept my mind swimming and my head in a
spin. So beautiful they were so way back when, they
kept me up dreaming of which one I'd win.
As I grew older, that young boy became a man and
my thoughts turned different directions and had
many more plans.
My heroes were the likes of Sir Winston, Harry,
Ronald and George. Their great contributions
reshaped this world and helped move us all
forward.
Now as I look in the mirror a much different image I
see. Larger, grayer, and yes a few wrinkles.
But older and wiser looking back at me,
the image I see is Dad.
Strange, I don't think so.
He was always my hero...

Written for and in the memory of my Dad...

Furman H. Beck Sr.

ABOUT THE AUTHOR:

FURMAN H. BECK JR.

I Can Never Go Home

My father was born and raised in Portman Shoals. He lived there until the Corps of Engineers purchased all property in the Hartwell Lake basin. He took his first steps at Portman. He made his first friends there. His first kiss was there. His first job was there. His values for life were established there. His sense of pride was poured into me there by my elders. He attended Zion Elementary and then went to Pendleton High School for one year before transferring to Anderson Boys High.

He lived there until 1957 when everyone had to move out. His roots ran deep then and they still do today.

Reluctantly he moved to Anderson with my grandparents, but home for him was still that little frame house sitting on a red clay hill in Portman.

He made friends, found a good church and did his very best to make this area his new home.

He graduated from Anderson Boys High in 1960, joined the SC Army National Guard and was honorably discharged six years later. He found the love of his life, my mother, Linda Woolbright, got married and in August of 2013 they will celebrate their 50th wedding anniversary. God blessed Mom and Dad with 3 children, Suzanne, Sharon & Benjamin (Benji) and 3 grandchildren Marilyn, Graham and Ella. He worked in the grocery business for awhile and then spent 18 years with a company affiliated with the Textile industry.

When Textiles went South, he had to reinvent himself. He had a growing family, a stay at home mom and facing college in the near future. He tried several things, a stint in retail management and then went into real estate and was Broker in Charge for a national company for a number of years.

Throughout his career he has been blessed in many ways. He got to see a good part of the world, traveling most of our 50 States and touring the Far East, Japan, Taiwan and The Philippines.

Looking back over the years he didn't realize just what we had at Portman until it was all gone. He and I both never once heard it mentioned in school and how important a role that Portman played in modern technology. Anderson is called the Electric City because of a young Engineer by the name of Whitner who at 27 had a vision and made it a reality. Lake Hartwell is a magnificent accomplishment in a Hydro-Electric Power generating plant, but it all started on a very small scale in a little village called, Portman Shoals...

No he can never go home, but he still has all the memories which his thoughts and his love for a very special place will forever be in his heart. He is now retired and spends his time on the farm fishing from the pond, spending time with his grandkids and writing. The name "Beck" literally means, "By the Water." Though his home by the river will forever be under water, the water will always be near him and he will forever be my hero... I am blessed through the years to be able to begin to see his image in the mirror looking back at me...

Benjamin (Benji) Furman Beck

Furman and Benji

Chris, Graham, Furman and Benji

Furman and Benji

Furman H. Beck Jr.

Furman and Linda with the Grandkids (Marilyn, Graham and Ella)

Linda with all the Ladies (Suzanne, Kristie, Ella, Marilyn and Sharon)

Furman with Whiskers the White Billy Goat's Grandson!

Coming Soon!

Portman Shoals:

The Forgotten Settlement

Revised Edition 2

Much more history on W.C. Whitner, Nikola Tesla, Hydro-Electric Power, Lake Hartwell Dam and how Portman Shoals helped pave the way for milestone accomplishments to take place in the United States and around the world like Niagara Falls!

Long distance transmission of electrical power was con-
ceived and first made a reality by W.C. Whitner in 1894 by a
power plant he designed at High Shoals on the Rocky River
near Anderson, SC. Upon his meeting with another like-
minded genius , Nikola Tesla , he was convinced his plan
would work and went on to create a Hydro-Electric Plant that
could produce 200 electrical horsepower from 5,000-volt generators. This was the first successful long distance transmission of electricity in the South.

Due to this success, Stanley Electric Company (now General
Electric Company) agreed to build 10-thread, 10,000 volt generators for Mr. Whitner and advised him that these were the
first built anywhere in the world for this type of commercial
use! Soon 11,000 volt generators began being built which gave
ground-breaking hydroelectric power plants like "Niagara
Falls," the ability to transmit long distance hydro-electric energy and forever change the world. The Portman Shoals Power
Plant on Nov. 1, 1897 began lighting homes and powering
business's for miles around even crossing state lines, making
it the first hydro-electric plant to produce high voltage power
without the need for help from step-up transformers in the
United States and quite possibly the world! It was also the first
in the world to create a cotton gin operated from electricity.
Hence, Anderson, SC became known as, "The Electric City."

Made in the USA
Charleston, SC
16 December 2012